# The Yoyo Dad's Journal:

## Raising Emotionally Healthy Kids in and Up and Down World

John T. Wu, Ed. D

ISBN:1478305770
ISBN-13:9781478305774

# CONTENTS

# ACKNOWLEDGMENTS

Cover Design by Libby Tipton
Ebook Formatting by Teresa L.C. Wu
Print Formatting by Natasha E. Wright
Edited by Kaitlin Barr Nadal
Website Design by Dr. Geoff Hsu

JOHN T. WU

# INTRODUCTION

I was nearly 30 years old when my first son was born. Though I was a Harvard-trained psychologist, I was shocked by how unprepared I was. I read the What to Expect When You Are Expecting books, my wife and I attended birthing classes, I talked to friend. . . some of it helped, but most of it was for naught. Everyone was well meaning, but the problem was that I wanted to know what to do with MY child, right NOW!

The problem with any writing on parenting or raising healthy kids is the same:

What do I do with MY child right NOW? I doubt this writing series will answer your particular questions. All I can do is share some of the key lessons I have learned as a professor who teaches child and adolescent development, as a counselor with nearly twenty years' experience with young adults, and as the father of two boys. I hope my experiences offer some guidelines and perspective as you decide how to handle your own kids.

I want to thank Teresa, my wife of 20 years, for sharing the parenting voyage with me. Most of all I want to thank my two boys, Nicholas and Zachary, for being fantastic kids whom I adore with all my heart. I also want to thank them for offering their yoyo skills for the videos seen at
www.yoyodad.com.

# CHAPTER 1
# DEADLY WORDS

When my kids were in elementary and middle school, we started playing the yoyo. Not the old fashioned yoyo of my youth, where doing tricks like the Sleeper or Around the World were pinnacles of achievement. The new-style yoyos of today now come complete with bearings, response systems, and advanced size and shape specifications. Across the months, we cheered as we learned Brain Twister, Eli Hops, Kwijibo, and eventually harder tricks like Superman and White Buddha. We also started collecting yoyos, first plastic, then metal ones, in colors that spanned the rainbow. . . green, blue, orange, and ones with acid wash and mottled finishes. Now, spending even a brief moment near us will provide a frenzied view of spinning and whirling yoyos.

After half a year of playing, guided only by yoyoexpert.com tutorials, our family drove hours north to our first yoyo competition. What a shock to see yoyoers of all ages and skill! Competitions usually consist of two parts. The first part is the freestyle event, where a player has one minute to perform whatever tricks he chooses (there are occasional females, but for some reason this sport is overwhelmingly male.) Freestylers are usually advanced players who have great technical skill and all seem to wear black t-shirts. The second part is the ladder division, where younger, less skilled players do a prescribed set of tricks of increasing difficulty until they fail two tricks in a row. My guys were capable of doing the ladder tricks but were intimidated and shy. Resisting our efforts to encourage (read: coerce) them to enter, I finally blurted out, "If you do it, I'll do it!"

So that is how I found myself at the front of an amphitheater, waiting to perform tricks in front of the professional judge panel and audience. The order was by age and the first player was 7 years old. I knew I had a long wait. My youngest son was soon called, and he coolly walked up and completed nearly every trick! Right before my oldest son was called up, the promotional yoyo he received for entering, and the one he planned to use in the competition, broke! They called his name and he looked at me with wild eyes. I silently handed him my yoyo. Without any practice or warm up, he proceeded to complete every trick in the ladder!

I was so happy for them that I was a bit startled when they called my name. "John Wu, age, uh...old." The crowd fell silent as I came up and addressed Judge Bill.

"My kids were shy, I said I would if they would, and so. . . here I am."

Somehow, that struck a chord with the other yoyo parents, and to my surprise, the crowd began to cheer for my tricks, no matter how simple or inept. And inept I was. I have talked imminently suicidal people into having hope. I have walked into hostile fraternities to give alcohol safety workshops. Never was I more nervous than I was at that moment. And yet, as I completed tricks like Walk the Dog, Rock the Baby, and Elevator, the cheering grew. Finally, I reached my maximum number of missed tricks and walked off the stage, amid cascading applause.

What really surprised me was what followed. Throughout the rest of the competition, wherever I went, people would come up and congratulate me for participating. A 90-year-old man stopped me and reminisced about yoyos "in his day." When we entered a pizza joint, a table of people pointed to me and clapped. Later, a little girl, no more than 5 or 6, approached me solemnly and spoke slowly, as if to a young child, "You tried very hard and did a good job." For a moment I thought she was going to pat me on the head. For some reason, my lack of skill, and willingness to do something I clearly wasn't good at, captured people's attention (or perhaps pity), and they responded with warmth and genuine encouragement.

This celebration of effort is the same thing we must do with our kids, because when we don't, we risk destroying their ability to rebound in the face of failure.

* * *

A student I had a while ago was a senior in biology whose hope had been to go to medical school. Unfortunately, by the time I met her, she was taking the same biology course for the third time and needed to pass so she could graduate. In tears, she told me that she didn't understand what had happened to her.

"When I was in high school, I was the valedictorian. Other students came to me for tutoring! Everyone knew I was the best. Now, I can't even pass this class. How did I go from being so smart. . . to being so dumb?"

Sadly, my student was struggling because of deadly words she had heard when she was young. There are many poisonous words that parents can say to kids: "You have no hope," "You are stupid," "How did you get so ugly?" (Uh, maybe genetics?). But these particular words are especially insidious, because while they masquerade as something positive, ultimately they are destructive. Are you ready? What could be so damaging? It is these three words:

"You are smart."

Smart? Isn't that a compliment? Well, not really. A psychologist named Carol Dweck did an interesting experiment. Imagine you are a 4- or 5-year-old child. You come into a room with a variety of puzzles and are allowed to play with them. Some are easy (think jigsaw puzzles), while some are quite difficult. Truthfully, they aren't difficult; they are impossible. Imagine solving those jigsaw puzzles with some of their pieces removed or switched with other puzzles. No matter how hard you try, you cannot complete these dastardly puzzles! After a set time, you are told that you can play with any puzzle you want for a while and are left alone. Of course, you should know that in a psychology experiment, when you think you are alone, you are never alone. Someone is always watching! Which puzzle do you choose to play with: the easy or the impossible puzzle? Roughly a third of the young kids chose the easy puzzle, even though they had just solved it.

Dweck pondered these findings and several that followed, and she created two descriptions of achievement attitudes. She labeled the kids who sought out the difficult puzzle as displaying Mastery Orientation. The Mastery kids stayed positive in the face of failure and expected future success. This led them to seek out challenge and not fear failure. The kids who wanted to redo the easy puzzle displayed a Helpless Orientation. The helpless kids felt sad and disappointed in the face of failure. They expressed doubt that they would ever be able to solve the puzzle, and ultimately, they avoided challenge and possible disappointment.

So what does this have to do with those dangerous words "You are smart?" When Dweck looked at 10-year-old kids, the difference in Mastery and Helpless kids became more apparent. Mastery kids believed that intelligence can grow and that success comes from effort. Helpless kids believed that intelligence was fixed and that success comes from ability. So when a parent tells a child "You are smart" (which most of us American parents are very quick to do), the well-meaning parent is ultimately building a helpless mindset in the child. When you succeed, it is because you are naturally smart. And the corollary is that because you are smart, things should come easy. Well, that works great when the work is simple, but it gives you nowhere to go once you face failure. And life is tough enough that eventually everyone faces failure in some way. A mastery viewpoint allows you face failure and then say, "I need to work harder," "I had better study more," or "I must practice again," rather than "I must not be good at this, I'll just stop."

When my son Nicholas was 5, he played in his first season of soccer. He, like all 5-year-old boys, decided that the only thing that mattered was scoring goals. And by the middle of the season, he was quite sad because though he tried very hard, he had not scored any goals. One day we were watching a pro soccer game on television where the winning team had won 1-0, and a graphic appeared that changed everything.

It showed that the winning team had 10 shots on goal.

"Nicholas, did you see that?" I cried. He was puzzled.

"Did you see the team that won the game?"

"Yes."

"Well, the team that won kicked the ball 10 times at the goal, and it only went in once! Buddy, we are going about your soccer game all wrong. Instead of counting how many times the ball goes in the goal, let's count how many hard kicks at the goal you can have! How many hard kicks at the goal do you think you can muster in your next game?"

He wasn't convinced, but I told him I would count the number of hard kicks at the goal, rather than the goals themselves. By the end of the game, he had more than 12 hard kicks at the goal, and amazingly, he scored four goals! Everyone was cheering wildly for him, and his coach ran up and down the sidelines yelling, "Who's the best soccer player in the world?!!" When he finally left his cheering teammates and coach, and approached me, I was filled with pride! But I had to be careful what I said next.

"I'm so proud of you, buddy. You had 12 hard kicks at the goal! And four of them went in! Running so hard to get more kicks at the goal really paid off!"

You see, by praising his effort (running and kicking), which he could control, rather than praising his accomplishment (a scored goal), which is often out of a person's control, it showed him how to act for success. And in those days when the ball wasn't going through the goal, he now knew how to cope with failure: Run harder, and kick more.

When kids get praised for being smart, they soak it up, and it makes them feel good as long as they succeed. But once they face difficulty or failure, then the kids are stuck. They are left thinking that they aren't smart any more, or that they are "just not good at this." Simply trying hard, repeatedly, is the success secret in most things. Praising a child's effort, especially when the child has success, creates a long-term blueprint for success. Dr. John Medina highlights the importance of effort in his wonderful Brain Rules books, and illustrates this vividly in the parenting video "Praising IQ" at his website www.brainrules.com.

I have worked in universities for over 20 years, and a tragic situation I see repeated over and over are students who start college full of hope and then fail out in their first year. Very often, their story is this: They stopped going to class, they turned in assignments late, and then they skipped or took the final unprepared. What is also striking is that often these kids are labeled "smart" and "full of potential" if only they tried. Frequently, their high school academic profile is a high SAT score with a non-stellar grade point average. The students themselves will often lament that they don't know why they don't work harder.

From my perspective, the reason these students procrastinate, skip class, and don't truly apply themselves is that they are protecting their self-image. By not trying, everyone still views them as smart. But to work hard and only get a C or a B is to call that into question. Many of these students would rather fail and be called lazy than truly try but not achieve well, and thus, in their eyes, prove themselves "dumb."

I will always remember Zac's first soccer team. The league was so desperate for coaches, they were recruiting the most unqualified, inept, unknowledgeable parents to run teams. That is how my wife and I became the coaches of the Yellow Spark 5-year-olds. Our team had nice boys, but frankly, every time a kid would kick the ball, he would stop, turn toward the stands, and pose for the resulting picture. I would gesture wildly and bellow, "Kick the ball again!" That became my coaching motto, and under my excellent leadership, the

Yellow Sparks worked valiantly, and lost every game.

By the middle of the season, it was clear that coaching does matter. Losing became our expectation. More importantly, I had a team of good-hearted boys who were highly discouraged and ready to give up. Remembering what worked with Nicholas, I called a team meeting.

"Boys, we are going to try something new. Forget the score. We are going to count and keep track of how many hard kicks you can have in a game."

I recruited Nicholas to be my statistician, and every time a kid kicked the ball cleanly, he got a point. More importantly, he learned that he could get a lot of points if he just kept running and kicked the ball again. During halftime at our next game, I greeted the boys as they came off the field.

"Jack, great job! You have eight hard kicks this half. Can you give me eight more?"

"Josh, you had four hard kicks. Good work. I want you to get even more this half."

And so on.

I told each kid how many hard kicks they had, and they were amazed at their prowess. Finally, at the end of the match, I announced to the team that they had more than 40 hard kicks that game, and the boys broke out in delirium! We had won that game by goals, but somehow that didn't matter. Our guys began to run hard, kick, and eventually pass to one another. We started climbing in the standings, and even in games we lost, our guys were exuberant. The other team would taunt:

"We won 3 to 2! Nah, Nah, we are better than you!"

Our guys would respond, "We had 47 hard kicks! Forty-seven is more than 3!"

The other team would walk away in confused defeat, because even when you are 5 years old, you know that 47 is a lot more than 3.

By the season's end, we played in the playoffs and won third place overall. I was incredibly proud of our Yellow Sparks' performance, and most of all, win or lose, of their finding the ultimate secret to a resilient lifestyle: Run hard, keep trying, and kick the ball again.

Chapter Keys:

* Praising a child's effort, especially when the child has success, creates a long-term blueprint for success.

* A mastery viewpoint allows you face failure and then say, "I need to work harder," "I had better study more," or "I must practice again," rather than "I must not be good at this, I'll just stop."

* "I'm so proud of you, buddy. You had 12 hard kicks at the goal! And four of them went in! Running so hard to get more kicks at the goal really paid off!"

* Many of these students would rather fail and be called lazy, than truly try but not achieve well, and thus, in their eyes, prove themselves "dumb."

JOHN T. WU

# CHAPTER 2
# NO MT

Her car swerved in erratic bursts as she jerked the steering wheel. Her silver SUV skittered on the road like a drop of water splashed in hot oil. She was trying to be discreet, but as my friend drove past her, what I saw confirmed my suspicions: She clutched her phone high as she struggled to text and drive.

The 2008 crash of a Southern California commuter train in which 25 people died and more than 100 people were injured was an especially somber event. Investigators believe that the engineer, who ran a red light, was text messaging at the critical moment of the accident.

Why do people do such dangerous things? I don't think it is because they are bad people or they are trying to be reckless. Ultimately, I think it comes down to people not understanding something fundamental about our brains: The brain does not multitask. No MT!

Okay, I know that even as you read this page your heart beats, your head nods in agreement, and you breathe repeatedly without any extra effort. That is not what I mean. I mean that the brain can handle only one attention-rich task at a time. Have you ever noticed that when you get lost and aren't sure where you are going, most often you turn down the radio, or that when you are trying hard to remember something, you close your eyes? When my wife and I are talking while we drive and the topic turns to serious matters, I often focus more and more of my attention on our conversation until, inevitably, I hear the words "Wasn't that our exit?" Or sadly, the opposite will happen, and I will tune out of our conversation to attend to the road, and then utter her least favorite phrase: "Could you repeat that?" The brain can accommodate only one attention-rich task at a time.

I often have my students conduct the following experiment. They break into pairs and make little balls of paper (hopefully not from their notes). Then, while one person recites something he or she knows by heart (the Pledge of Allegiance, a poem, the Lord's Prayer), the other person begins to toss the little balls to them. When the tosses are slow and arcing, the reciter can keep up the recitation. But once the balls begin to speed up and the reciter has less time, the pledge becomes interrupted, halting, and less smooth. "I pledge allegiance...to the flag. . . of the United States of America." It also will become rushed in between throws: "andtotherepublicforwhichitstands. . ."

What is going on? Your brain has a primary focus of attention, and when something competes for its attention, it has to put down what it is doing, pick up the new task, and then reverse it and switch back. Literally, as the little balls come to you, your brain switches its focus from reciting, to catching, and then back again. And in between catches, it tries to jam as much of the reciting as possible before having to switch again. It is like working with only one arm. When you want to pick something up, you have to put down the object you are holding, pick up the new item, then reverse. And that picking up and putting down has a cost of both time and energy.

Further, when you focus on something, your brain will actually increasingly ignore the things just outside that focus. This phenomenon is how magicians can so successfully conduct sleight of hand tricks right in front of you. A magician shows you a coin, and then, as he holds up his other hand, the coin seems to transfer magically from one hand to the next. Of course, we know there are two coins and that the magician is hiding one as he shows the other. But as he palms the extra coin, it is not just that the hand is faster than the eye, but that the brain doesn't register what the eye sees if the magician can direct your attention somewhere else. (This is also why autistic people are less easily fooled by magic tricks. They do not catch the social cues a magician uses to manipulate audience attention, such as a glance elsewhere, looking up and smiling, or holding a different object up. Thus, they are more likely to see and register the palming of the coin.)

This is why driving while using a cell phone is so dangerous. Talking on a cell phone while driving impairs your reaction time as much as being legally drunk. Whoa, can that really be true? If you have people in the car with you, you can talk with them and not be impaired (at least, if you are not a new driver with lots of rowdy peers in the back distracting you). But if you are talking on a cell phone while driving, your brain has to focus somewhere outside of the actual driving environment. If you are telling Aunt Millie what you had for dinner and a dog runs out in front of your car, kiss Fido good-bye.

A lot of folks misunderstand this data to mean that the problem is that their hands are occupied, so they feel relieved they are responsibly using a hands-free headset. Unfortunately, they don't understand how the brain works. Here is the truth: It is not the manipulating of the phone that causes the impairment—it is the brain's primary focus being on something other than the road. A wireless headset frees the hands, but not the brain! If your brain is focused elsewhere, to recognize a significant driving threat you have to put down your conversation, pick up the threat, and then take driving action. Meanwhile, your car continues to barrel down the road. Be careful, Fido!

But what about having people in the car with you and talking to them? Does that impair you as much as a phone conversation? It seems like it should, but it doesn't. I carpool regularly to work, so I have the experience of talking in the car all the time. When I am telling my carpool buddy what I did over the weekend while he is driving, if another car begins to drift our way, my story slows. If there is a sudden slowing of traffic, I might gasp and stop talking. And if it is extreme, I might actually point out the traffic situation: "Whoa, that woman is weaving all over the road. I bet she is on her cell phone!" When you talk with someone in person, you naturally modulate the flow of information to fit the environment. If I were telling the same story to my carpool buddy by phone, I would happily continue with my story, oblivious to the changing driving threats around him. All in all, Fido much prefers that you talk to me in person, not on the phone.

Of course, if talking on a cell phone is bad, you can imagine how much worse actually trying to text on a cell phone is. Now my hands and brain are occupied with something other than driving, and I am going to react much more slowly than I would if I were unimpaired. What about listening to the radio or a book on tape? Does that impair my driving? Surprisingly not. The key is that you don't have to respond to those things, so you feel free to shift your attention back and forth.

I have a friend with very long legs who used to enjoy putting both hands behind his head as he held the steering wheel with his knees. He especially delighted in driving past people on the freeway and waving with both hands as he passed by. Other people would stare at him with accusing glares, clearly thinking, "What an irresponsible driver!" Yet they would think nothing of then picking up their cell phones and calling their friends to complain, never recognizing the irony of their similar impairment.

So how does this affect kids, especially when they can't drive yet? It turns out inattentive walking is also dangerous! The University of Alabama conducted a study asking children to cross a street in a simulator. They found that when using a cell phone, the children were 43% more likely to be hit or nearly hit by a vehicle. As children receive cell phones at earlier and earlier ages, the importance of having them pay attention in dangerous situations is clear.

This primary concept, that the brain doesn't multitask, is one that kids can apply to their academic life. When you study, focus on studying. Do not do it in front of the TV. A 2011 Boston College study found that when given a computer and television, the average subject estimated that they switched their gaze back and forth 15 times in half an hour. When the researchers analyzed the data using high-speed cameras, they found the average amount of switching was 120 times. We are extremely poor at estimating our own distraction! When your child tells you, "I'm not really watching the TV," she is not purposefully lying, but she is still quite wrong.

What about listening to music when you study? If you must have music, listening to something that doesn't have words like classical or jazz is better than music with lyrics. And no social media! Dr. Larry Rosen reports that middle school, high school, and college-aged students who check their Facebook accounts once a day have overall lower grades. Trying to study while your phone or computer notifies you that you have a Facebook update, or text, or new email means divided attention. And divided attention leads to weak learning. Every time your computer produces the little "ding" that means you have a new message, it forces you to put down what you are doing, pick up that piece of info, and then come back to studying. The modern portrait of studying, a kid with music blaring, the TV in the background, and a smart phone next to him as he "studies" is rife with distractions, and, ultimately, the kid will have to work much harder and longer to learn that material than if he had just focused on it the first time.

In 2009, Drs. Ophir and Nass, two Stanford researchers, conducted a study contrasting heavy multitaskers with light multitaskers. Surprisingly, they found that chronic multitaskers were worse at switching tasks than light multitaskers, even though they had more practice. In other words, those who tried to multitask the most were the least successful! But while the heavy multitaskers did worse, they rated multitasking as more pleasurable. I think this is the real danger of the multi-tasking world we live in. Like fast food, TV, and other pleasures of our modern age, they feel good, but they aren't good for you. Consequently, we are creating a generation of chronically stimulated youth who mistake arousal for learning and comprehension.

To learn something, remember that the brain handles one attention-rich task at a time, so focus on one thing at a time. And parents, stop using the phone while driving, especially when your kids are in the car. Fido says thank you.

Chapter Keys:

* The brain can handle only one attention-rich task at a time.

* A wireless headset frees the hands, but not the brain!

* Divided attention leads to weak learning.

* Those who tried to multitask the most were the least successful! But while the heavy multitaskers did worse, they rated multitasking as more pleasurable.

# CHAPTER 3
# BUILD A BETTER BRAIN

My boys will tell you that their parents are a bit odd. While many Asian parents frequently tell their kids to study, in our house, our kids are more likely to hear:

"Run in the canyon."

"Shoot some baskets."

"How many push-ups can you do?"

While it might seem like we have our hearts set on athletic scholarships, the real reason we have always emphasized a sound body in our home is because it is good for the brain. When you are developing and are young, your brain thrives on the oxygen-rich blood that flows to it after your body works hard. Dr. Michelle Voss recently reviewed more than 100 articles on the impact of exercise on the brain and found that at an early age, exercise improves attention, memory, and decision making, and at a later age, it improves planning, inhibition (a positive thing that keeps you from saying embarrassing things to your boss), and the ability to anticipate and respond to changing situations. Research even indicates exercise enlarges certain brain structures!

When school districts are facing budget shortages, they often consider cutting items like sports and PE. Instead, they should be adding more time for these activities because they actually promote better behavior and improved learning. Not to mention that they provide the magic words in these metric-obsessed times: higher test scores!

A wonderful book that examines the many advantages of exercise for your brain is Spark, by John Ratey and Eric Hagerman. They describe the Naperville school district in Illinois, which has made personal fitness one of the key features of its academic philosophy. By using heart monitors and rewarding time spent in healthy heart ranges, the district has taken away the competitive aspects of exercise and the idea that only one person can be a winner. So while several kids might run around a track, the fast, smooth-running jock who finishes first might actually be working less intensely than the clumsy, awkward kid who stumbles in toward the end. Why do this? The schools found tests scores increased throughout the district, and, indeed, in the Trends in International Mathematics and Science Study that looks at achievement inter-nationally, the Naperville 8th graders scored first in the world in science knowledge.

So does that mean your kids should study while they run around the track? No, of course not! They would look silly, and other kids would laugh at them. In another study, subjects were asked to learn things while they were working out hard, and guess what? They did poorly. This makes sense when you realize that all the blood is shunted from the extremities (like the brain) to the major muscle groups. The key is what happens afterwards. Your heart is pushing all this blood as fast as possible around your body so that your big muscles have oxygen. Once you slow down, your brain can soak up all that extra fuel and oxygen to operate at its best. You can see why, before a big test, it might be wise to jog around the track once or twice. (Zac, you might remember how your 4th grade teacher would make your class run before the big standardized tests? …Uh, yeah, that was my fault. Sorry about that.)

So why does exercise improve cognitive performance so strongly? Your brain is infinitely complex, and what makes it so complicated are not just the 100 billion brain cells that you have, but the thousands of connections each neuron makes with other ones. When you exercise, you produce more of a magical substance called BDNF, which stimulates the growth of those neuron connections. Also, when you exercise, you produce more neurons. Running around during recess, playing soccer, or riding a bike stimulates both neuron production and neuron connections. Yes, a percentage of the new neurons die off, and exercise doesn't change that percentage, but because you produce more neurons to begin with, you get to keep more in the long run. Thus, exercise leads to a bigger and better brain!

Another big benefit to you when you exercise is that your brain produces a host of neurotransmitters. Your cells communicate with one another by sending these neuro-chemicals across a small gap between neurons called a synapse. When enough of the transmitters make it across the gap, the next cell fires (and those transmitters have to avoid being sucked up by the original neuron or attacked and dismantled by enzymes in the gap before finding the appropriate landing spot, sort of like a Hunger Games version of musical chairs).

Different neurotransmitters do different things in the brain. Some make brain circuits fire; some cause brain circuits to slow down. This balance of having all the different parts of the brain operate cohesively is much like a well-run orchestra, where each section knows its music and plays in the right rhythm and volume with the other sections. Sometimes, one section decides to go rogue, and during the performance, the trumpets stand up and start playing twice as fast and as loud as they can. Meanwhile, the percussion section has gotten sleepy and is hitting beats slow and weakly. Having the right balance of neurotransmitters is like having a good conductor who can calm down the trumpets and wake up the percussionists.

Exercise not only ups the amount of neurotransmitters—it does so in the correct proportions so that you get beautiful music throughout your head. This is why someone who is depressed and slow, and someone who is hyperactive and can't focus, both benefit when they exercise. That is also why really experienced teachers send their kids to run around outside when the class is out of sorts, and right before a big exam.

Okay, so how much exercise do you need? Well, the short answer is, probably more than most kids are doing now. Something is better than nothing, and usually more is better than less. Every day you should run, shoot baskets, ride bikes, or do something aerobic for half an hour to an hour. A couple of times a week you need to really work hard, sprint, play full court basketball, or play soccer to truly benefit your body and mind. Duncan Buchan and his associates contrasted two groups of high school adolescents who exercised either in long 20-minute runs or in four to six sprints of 20 meters. At the end of seven weeks, while the long running group exercised longer and expended nearly five times more calories, both groups had similar improvements in aerobic fitness and reduced body fat. If you don't have time for a long workout, a short high-intensity workout still can be beneficial.

Dr. Daniel Amen states that the best sports are the ones where you have to think while you move. Thus, tennis and basketball are better for your brain than simple running or swimming. But sports that involve blows to the head, like boxing and football, are likely to have long-term negative consequences, as a lifetime of stressing and straining your neuron axons causes them to become inflamed and function less effectively. Dr. Amen recently completed a study of retired NFL players and found significant damage to their brains that often led to depression and cognitive problems. What about soccer? It is a great game, except for striking the ball with your head. In his book Magnificent Mind at Any Age, Amen quotes a University of Cincinnati College of Medicine study that found reduced gray matter in male college soccer players compared with those who had never played.

My sons might remember that in youth soccer, when the ball would go in the air, many parents would yell "Head it," while one frantic dad screamed "Run away! Protect your brain!" Well, I won't reveal his identity, but let's just say it is possible he had a yoyo in his pocket.

Exercise—your brain will thank you. And the next time you see your doctor, you might want to ask, "Doc, did you work out this morning? I need your brain to be at its best!"

Chapter Keys:

* Exercise leads to a bigger and better brain!

* Exercise not only ups the amount of neurotransmitters—it does so in the correct proportions so that you get beautiful music throughout your head.

* If you don't have time for a long workout, a short-high intensity workout still can be beneficial.

* The best sports are the ones where you have to think while you move.

# Chapter 4
# FANTASTIC FATHERS

My last topic is one that is dear to my heart: Dads matter! We live in a society that frequently puts fathers down. Television comedies rarely show caring, capable, strong fathers. Instead, the portrayal is more often a childish, immature, buffoonish dad who adds to the burden of his competent, long-suffering wife. Children's books also tend to leave dads out or make them minor characters. (I remember gritting my teeth whenever I would read the Berenstain Bears series with their constantly inept father.) I assume the intent is to make children without fathers avoid feeling left out, but an unintended consequence is minimizing the importance of fathers.

While there is a host of research about children and mothers, the research on fathers is more sparse. What we do know is that fathers interact differently with children than mothers do. Certainly a child will attach to a dad as easily as a mom, given consistent and warm interactions while young. But even so, fathers are not just mothers with a bit of stubble on their chin.

Dads tend to play more physically with their kids. If you are walking through a crowded mall and happen to see a baby tossed in the air laughing with glee, odds are high it is a dad catching the child. According to Jeffrey Rosenberg and Bradford Wilcox, in their 2006 summary of the impact of fathers on children's well-being, positive fathers, described as "involved, nurturing, and playful," teach children how to regulate aggression and display self-control through this rough style of play. These kids are also more likely to explore and display confidence and independence. As they grow older, kids with positive relationships with their dads display better school behavior, less depression, and less drug use.

Rosenberg and Wilcox also describe a host of cognitive benefits for children with positive fathers, such as more advanced vocabulary, cognitive abil-ities, and IQs. These same kids display higher academic success in high school and have more positive peer relationships as well.

One of the most positive effects a father can have on a child is to love that child's mother. When constructive conflict reso-lution, respect, and empathy are modeled for children, they are less likely to grow up and participate in unhealthy and abusive relationships.

Several years ago, I heard Josh McDowell, a notable expert on youth, describe a study by Columbia University that so surprised me, I was convinced he quoted it inaccurately. It turns out he nailed it. The Center on Addiction and Substance Abuse (CASA) at Columbia University studied the impact of family structure and drug use in 1999, polling 2,000 adolescents aged 12 to 17 years old and 1,000 of their parents. Researchers found the smoking, drinking, and drug use of kids who lived with their mothers alone increased 30% when compared to kids from two-parent homes. But in two-parent homes where the father was distant from the family, researchers found a 68% increase in destructtive behavior, much more than in the single-parent homes! In two-parent homes where children had a good to excellent relationship with their father, incidences of smoking, drinking, and drug use dropped 94%. When both parents are in the home, and Dad is involved with the family, there was almost no way you could make the child go astray.

This study is a humbling one for me. Dads make a difference, but that difference can be positive or negative. While mothers provide high constant efforts toward their children regardless of life's circumstances, dads vary. And that variation changes a child's life profoundly.

I have been married for 20 years, and there are times when I feel pretty proud of that. However, this study indicates that it isn't enough just to stay married. It is how well I interact and engage with my wife and children that leads to good things in their lives. Rosenberg and Wilcox list seven dimensions of effective fathering:

- Fostering a positive relationship with the children's mother
- Spending time with children
- Nurturing children
- Disciplining children appropriately
- Serving as a guide to the outside world
- Protecting and providing
- Serving as a positive role model

I first noticed the impact of fathers during my college years. I was leading a group of junior high kids at my local church, and most of the time it was the blind leading the blind. But we had incredible group cohesion and unity because we really tried to care about everyone in the group (indeed, we titled ourselves NITELIGHT: Never In The Emptiness, Living In God's House Together). One factor that was paramount in whether a 6th grade kid would come and get involved in our group was the participation of the child's father. If the father was interested and involved in spiritual matters, then almost always, the child would join and become an integral part of our group. But if only the mom was spiritually focused, and dad was uninterested, the kid would often drift away.

It was this line of thinking that led me to change my career path. For the first 10 years of my psychology career, I worked full-time in university counseling centers. I counseled undergrads, graduate students, and their families. I consulted with university admini-strators on how to best meet the psychological needs of their students, and how to best console them after crises or emergencies. I supervised and trained young doctoral students, I gave educational workshops all over campus, and I worked with highly intelligent clients who tended to get better. All in all I loved it.

And in 2001 I left it behind.

With 3-year-old and 1-year-old sons, I could see that the long work hours and constantly being on call was draining my energy and taking time from my own family. I decided to transition into full-time teaching and began to teach at a small, faith-based liberal arts college. Little did I know that I would deeply love my new campus and students, and what started as a sacrifice for the sake of my family led to my true calling and passion: educating a new generation of people helpers.

I am certainly not saying I am a perfect father. My boys, Father's Day cards notwithstanding, would be the first to tell you that. But I am a more present father, and we spend a lot of time together. Frankly, that is why I picked up the yoyo in the first place. Boys' relationships tend to be activity based, and if you sit down with a boy and ask him to talk to you, you'll typically get monosyllabic grunts. But interact with that boy, shooting baskets, building legos, or playing yoyo, and he will talk freely. By being around more, I am hoping to be in that third category of the CASA study.

My view of parenting now is like piloting a boat. Focused attention allows many small corrections to the rudder and a smooth journey for the passengers. Infrequent, sporadic steering, with large, violent turns of the tiller, leads to panic and dismay for those on board. Dads who hang around and get involved with their families often pilot their kids to a smoother journey through adolescence.

For young women, my message is to consider what sort of father a man will be before they get married. Remember the Pixar movie Finding Nemo? What if, ladies, you were to die and your child became lost? To what end would your future husband pursue your child? When you are dating, don't pay attention just to how this man treats you (If he can't treat you well, why are you with him?), but also how he treats the little people in his life: a harried server at a restaurant, a maid at a hotel, someone begging on a street corner. If he doesn't treat these people well, it is hard to imagine he will treat a crying infant, a whiny child, or a mouthy adolescent well. You can save yourself and your children a large amount of grief by choosing your mate wisely from the outset.

To men, my hope is that you will recognize the incredibly influential role you play in the lives of your families. Our culture says you aren't really very important. The data say that is a lie. Your families need you! Step into that responsibility and give it everything you have. Dads matter!

Chapter Keys:

* Certainly a child will attach to a dad as easily as a mom, given consistent and warm interactions while young. But even so, fathers are not just mothers with a bit of stubble on their chin.

* One of the most positive effects a father can have on a child is to love that child's mother.

* When both parents are in the home, and Dad is involved with the family, there was almost no way you could make the child go astray.

* Your families need you! Step into that responsibility and give it everything you have. Dads matter!

# CONCLUSION

When I try to learn a yoyo trick I go through several predictable stages. First, I am intrigued and amazed by the trick and say "I can't wait to learn this!" Next, I actually try the trick, become overwhelmed, and say "This is impossible!" Finally, I break the trick into small doable sequences, and slowly learn it piece by piece. Eventually, the trick becomes so smooth and effortless that I say, "What was the big deal in learning this?"

When it comes to parenting you may go through similar stages. The key is to persist and to break your goals into small doable chunks. Eventually, you will move past the frustration and the new skills and the focus you seek will become second nature. I hope these ideas about focusing on effort, single-tasking your attention, the brain building effects of exercise, and the importance of fathers have offered some tips and inspiration in how to care for and raise your children.

If you would like to discuss these topics or learn about further installments of this journal, follow me on Facebook at 'Yoyo Dad's Journal', twitter at @yoyodadsjournal, and view yoyo videos at this journal's website www.yoyodad.com. If you are in San Diego, California and wish to talk about your personal situation, feel free contact my private counseling practice at www.celebrationcounseling.com to set up an appointment.

Finally, if you are ever at a yoyo competition and see a gimpy, middle-aged

Asian guy standing on stage, please cheer him on no matter how pathetic he plays.

Blessings,
John Wu (aka The Yoyo Dad)

# REFERENCES

Amen, D. G. (2006). Making a good brain great: The Amen Clinic program for achieving and sustaining optimal mental performance. New York: Three Rivers Press.

Amen, D. G. (2008). Magnificent mind at any age. New York: Harmony Books.

Amen, D. G. (2011). Amen Clinics scores big with NFL study. Retrieved from http://70.32.73.82/blog/4560/amen-clinics-scores-big-with-nfl-study/

American Physiological Society (2011, July 25). Exercise has numerous beneficial effects on brain health and cognition, review suggests. ScienceDaily. Retrieved from http://www.sciencedaily.com-/releases/2011/07/110725132656.htm

American Psychological Association (2011, August 6). Social networking's good and bad impacts on kids. ScienceDaily. Retrieved from http://www.sciencedaily.com-/releases/2011/08/110806203538.htm

Boston College (2011, May 2). Media multitasking is really multi-distracting. ScienceDaily. Retrieved from http://www.sciencedaily.com-/releases/2011/05/110502084444.htm

Buchan, D. S., Stewart, O., Young, J. D., Thomas, N. E., Cooper, S.-M., Tong, T. K.,...& Baker, J. S. (2011). The effects of time and intensity of exercise on novel and established markers of CVD in adolescent youth. American Journal of Human Biology 23(4): 9.

Harwood, R., Miller, S. A., & Vasta, R. (2008). Child psychology development in a changing society. Hoboken, John Wiley & Sons.

Latham, C. (2006, Nov. 11). Why do you turn down the radio when you're lost? Sharpbrains. Retrieved from http://www.sharpbrains.com/blog/2006/1 1/11/why-do-you-turn-down-the-radio-when-youre-lost/

Medina, J. (2008). Brain rules: 12 principles for surviving and thriving at work, home, and school. Seattle: Pear Press.

Medina, J. (2010). Brain rules for baby: How to raise a smart and happy child from zero to five. Seattle: Pear Press.

National Center on Addiction and Substance Abuse at Columbia University (1999, August 30). CASA 1999 Teen/parent drug survey reveals: Dads AWOL in teen substance abuse battle. Press Releases: 1992-2000. Retrieved from http://test.casacolumbia.org/templates/PressReleases.aspx?articleid=140&zoneid=49

NOVA scienceNOW (2010, Dec. 2). Magic and autism. PBS.org. Retrieved from http://www.pbs.org/wgbh/nova/body/magic-autism.html

Ophir, E., Nass, C., et al. (2009). Cognitive control in media multitaskers. Proceedings of the National Academy of Sciences of the United States of America 106(37): 15,583-15,587.

Ratey, J. J., & Hagerman, E. (2008). Spark:
The revolutionary new science of exercise
and the brain. New York: Little, Brown.

Rosen, C. (2008). The myth of multitasking.
New Atlantis: A Journal of Technology &
Society 20: 105-110.

Rosenberg, J., & Wilcox, W. B. (2006). The
importance of fathers in the healthy
development of children. Office on Child
Abuse and Neglect, U.S. Children's
Bureau. Retrieved from
http://www.childwelfare.gov/pubs/userm
anuals/fatherhood/

University of Alabama at Birmingham (2009,
January 27). Cell phones dangerous for
child pedestrians, study finds.
ScienceDaily. Retrieved from
http://www.sciencedaily.com-
/releases/2009/01/090126112429.htm

# OTHER YOYO DAD MATERIAL

Yoyo Dad 2: Dating Well in an Up and Down World.
Visit Amazon.com to buy a copy.

Visit
www.yoyodad.com
for information about the author and yoyo video clips.